JOURNEY TO RESURRECTION

The Drama of Lent and Easter in the Gospel of John

Richard Simon Hanson

PAULIST PRESS
New York/Mahwah

Copyright © 1986
by Richard Simon Hanson

All rights reserved. No part of this book may be reproduced or transmitted in any form, or by any means, electronic or mechanical including photocopying, recording or by any information storage and retrieval system without permission in writing from the Publisher.

Library of Congress
Catalog Card Number: 85-62045

ISBN: 0-8091-2737-7

Published by Paulist Press
997 Macarthur Boulevard
Mahwah, New Jersey 07430

Printed and bound in the
United States of America

Contents

	Introduction	1
	The Prelude to the Signs	3
One	The Sign of the Wine	5
Two	The Sign of the Temple	11
Three	The Sign of the Well	18
Four	The Sign of the Healer	24
Five	The Sign of the Bread	31
Six	The Sign of Sight	37
Seven	The Sign of the Tomb	44

Eight
　　The Passion 51

Nine
　　Resurrection Morn 67

Supplement
　　Directions for Staging as Chancel Drama 71

Introduction

The Gospel according to John is unlike the other Gospels. Those other three, Mark and Matthew and Luke, are known as the Synoptic Gospels because of certain similarities they have in common. It is as though they follow a basic story, represented best by Mark's Gospel, that is expanded by the other two with material that Mark did not know. It is all more complicated than that, of course, but that is what seems readily apparent.

John's Gospel stands apart—in plot, in material, in style. It is a testimony all by itself. Selecting material rather than collecting all that was available, John and his followers presented a series of testimonies that define and proclaim the chief character in his story. Some of those testimonies have a particular form that John calls a *sign*.

These "signs," apparently seven but possibly eight in number, succeed in combining what come out as two sets of materials in the three Synoptic Gospels: the miracles and the parables.

Contrary to what seems to be a common understanding of them, the signs in John's Gospel are not simply miracles. They are miracles told as lessons or proclamations. Each sign has the effect of a parable, that is. Each sign becomes a springboard for strong and important statements of Jesus that explain who he was and what he was trying to do. Each sign becomes a teaching of the Master.

Various people have noticed the dramatic quality of these prominent episodes called the signs in the Gospel of John. In my own teaching career I have tried to find ways to present them dramatically. On many occasions I have tried improvised dramas. Unrehearsed, my students have acted out the various parts in each sign. The result has been exciting. Each sign has "opened up" as we act it out. Indeed, I am convinced that they could be written as a series of chancel dramas for actual production. People properly trained in the theatre arts could produce very interesting and effective versions of these episodes. Short of that, it occurs to me that it will be helpful simply to think of them as dramatic in character and therefore I am here presenting something that might be called "drama in print." I shall narrate each episode as though it were being played out and then, at the end of this treatment, I shall add some suggestions for actual performance on stage or in chancel.

Whether cast as real drama or merely read with the eye, it is important that we visualize each of these episodes in turn, for without that visualization the lines will not have their full import. So I beg you, dear reader, to imagine the scenes in your head if you can't go so far as to act them out.

The Prelude to the Signs[1]

I am here to tell you of something primeval,
of something so basic, so elementary, so important,
that I must tell you it is our very beginning.
It is something of God,
something from God,
something that is the very expression of God from the
    beginning,
from before all that we know,
which brought all else into being.
It came to us as light in our darkness,
as life in the midst of our death and dying,
as truth to challenge all our deceptions,
and yet—as flesh and blood,
as a man who demands we believe him and trust him
as though he were sent from God himself.
Because he was.
He was born by the very will of God
and that is also the way that he lived.
Another man pointed him out. That man was John of
    the River Jordan.
"This one," said he, "is greater than I.
This one is so much greater than I

---

1. It is intended and advised that this prelude be read again prior to each of the episodes in the series, including the last great act.

that I am not worthy of tying his shoelace.
Behold him! He is God's sacrifice.
Behold him as Isaac,[2] the special son born to be laid on the altar.
This is God's lamb who has come to bring health and healing[3]
by taking away the ill of the world."
This man was God's truth,
come to penetrate and conquer our evil.
This was God's gift of kindness.
From the bosom of God he came to live among us
and his life was kindness and truth combined.

---

2. The important Greek word *monogenēs*, normally translated as "only-begotten," is also used to describe Isaac in the writings of Josephus, who was a contemporary of the New Testament writers.

3. The term "salvation" and its cognates was a term that really meant "health" and whatever words are cognate to that. The Roman emperors used that terminology often in their political propaganda, usually to mean the health of the economy.

One

The Sign of the Wine

The voice of my beloved!
Behold, he comes
leaping on the mountains,
bounding over the hills!
My beloved is a gazelle;
he is a young stag.
Behold, there he stands
behind our wall,
gazing in at the window,
looking through the screen!
   (words recited by the bride at an ancient wedding)

Arise, my love, my fairest!
Arise, come away!
Lo, the winter is past,
the rain is over and gone.
Flowers appear in the land.
The time for singing has come,
the voice of the turtledove calls,
the fig tree puts forth figs
and the vines are in bloom.
Arise, my love, my fairest!
Arise, come away!
   (words recited by the groom)

The first sign on the way is a wedding feast. It is a village affair, in Cana of Galilee. All the kinfolk of two Jewish families are there. There is music, perhaps even dancing. Dare we imagine an antiphony of men and women singing the stanzas that are still preserved in the Song of Songs?

Mary the wife of Joseph has been invited to this wedding feast. So also her son Jesus, who comes with his Galilean companions. As these enter they pause to notice six large stoneware jars. Those jars are the vessels used for the rituals of purification, the washing of hands for which good Jews were famous. One would assume, of course, that the jars contain water. Why else would they be standing there? These jars will turn out to be as important as any of the characters in this little drama. We might even imagine some comments about them as Jesus' friends enter with him.

"Look at those handsome jars, will you!"

"A faithful household for sure. But six jars only. If they had a full seven then they should be fulfilling the law to perfection."

"Do you suppose they draw from this water each day?"

We can imagine Jesus and his companions finding their place at the feast somewhere near his mother Mary. But let us not imagine something sedate. This is a true Middle Eastern affair with much laughter, singing, conversation, dancing, eating and drinking. We are part of a noisy crowd. Their intention is joy and pleasure. This must be a full celebration.

But suddenly we are aware that something has gone wrong. The sounds of joy have subsided. Embarrassing comments are being passed from one guest to another.

"I say, I would like some more wine!"

"More wine here, if you please."

"What? There isn't any more wine?"

The Sign of the Wine

"Well! They say that a man provides for a woman only as well as he can provide at the wedding feast. These folks aren't doing very well!"

"O dear, what a pity! Until now it was a respectable feast."

"Poor Josi! If his father can't do better than this for the wedding, how can he possibly manage to keep a wife?"

The revelry flags. Here and there people make an effort to be boisterous and merry but the spreading news of the shortage of wine is clearly blanketing the whole affair. The situation becomes more and more distressing as attention is focused on the bridegroom and his inability to provide. Mary picks up the embarrassment and registers it as she turns to look at her son. "My son," she says, "they have no wine."

"What does that matter for me?" he responds. Then there is a pause in which mother communicates to son something that he needs to understand. His response to what she says in that silence tells us that he did understand. "Mother," he says, "my hour has not yet come."

But Mary knows better. She knows that it has. Without further consulting him she walks over to a group of household servants and gives them orders as she gestures toward this son of hers. "You go to him and do what he says. Whatever he tells you to do, you do it. Do you understand?"

Do they understand? Doing what they are told is what they best understand, for these are household servants. Four or five of them approach Jesus. They are somewhat puzzled but they are willing. This man is not their master but it is their lot in life to obey.

"Do you see those large water vessels standing over there?"

They see them. Indeed they have been seeing them often as they have done their duties about this household.

"Fill them."

Of a sudden we know a secret: the stone jars were empty! There should have been water in them, but there is not. The jars are a pretense. They suggest that this family kept the tradition of Moses but now we discover that they do not. They are hypocrites who only pretend to keep their tradition. They have the form of it but not the content.

The servants, of course, are puzzled by the command. They are embarrassed. We can imagine that Jesus may have had to do more than merely say, "Fill the jars." He may have had to get them moving and hustle them along.

The filling of the jars is not an incidental scene in this little drama. It is extremely important. Unless the jars are filled with water, the miracle of the wine cannot take place. Unless the tradition of the prior age is fulfilled, the new age cannot come. One day must be completed before the next day can begin.

Each Gospel writer handled this message in his own way. Matthew recalled Jesus saying, "I came to fulfill the torah and the prophets." Luke spoke of the son who came to redeem the people of the Jewish tradition, to validate all they had lived and hoped for through the centuries. John does the same with the water jars. The empty jars betray an unfulfilled tradition, a covenant not completely kept. First that tradition must be fulfilled. First the Father's will for Israel would have to be done, all the way to the bitter cup. Only then could they taste the wine of new life, the wine of resurrection.

Having obeyed the command, the servants bring the water to the steward of the feast. Did they expect to be cuffed or severely reprimanded for such a jest as to bring water when wine was called for? Perhaps. But they were servants and servants must obey. Obedience came first for them as it would have to come for the nation and for Jesus. Only after obedience would the miracle occur. The servants pass jugs of water to the guests at the wedding feast. What else was there for the quenching of thirst than the water which Jesus commanded?

But lo, the second surprise of our drama! As the water is poured it comes out as fine wine. In the giving, in the offering of the water, the miracle occurs. To the servants' complete amazement the wedding guests are not only satisfied but overjoyed.

"Wine we have at last!"

"Taste this if you will. It's not half bad. Much better than what we had at first, I would say."

"A toast for the groom and his family! A toast for the wine itself! At every other feast the good wine is served first and then, when the guests have drunk 'til they don't know the difference, the cheaper wine is served. But you, sir—you are a provider beyond expectation. You have saved the finest wine until last. A toast, I say, to the bridegroom and to his father!"

The double meaning of the steward's words should not be lost. There are two bridegrooms here and a true Father. The first bridegroom fell short. He ran out of wine. The best he could provide became empty vessels, and the empty stone jars of his father's household portended that. But appears a truer Son and the party is saved. This one knows that empty jars must first be filled, then emptied in order to produce joy for all.

For that one, the task became clear. As his mother understood ahead of him, he would have to fulfill his people's tradition, then empty himself—offer himself as wine to the world. And in that offering he would rise. Joy would be fulfilled in his rising and the party could commence.

So we end it there. We end it as a new beginning. The drinking of the new wine produces more dancing and singing. The party is revived, yet with greater exuberance than before. The music is Joy to the World and Hail to the Brightness and Lo, He Comes. The music is Easter and Christmas combined.

The mood is hope as well as joy. The mood is promise. Here we see the first possibility of the dawn of a new age.

> Go forth, O daughter of Zion
> and behold King Solomon
> with the crown with which his mother crowned him
> on the day of his wedding,
> on the day of his gladness of heart.
> *(Song of Songs 3:11)*

Two

The Sign of the Temple

In the first episode Jesus discovered something about himself and his powers. In the second episode he discovers even more. As he beheld the temple in its grand reconstruction begun by King Herod, he found himself identifying with it. We shall never know exactly why he made his first trip to the temple but we can imagine that he came out of devotion, hoping to encounter his Father there. What he encountered in fact was something that disturbed him.

Let us imagine ourselves there with him or just watching. The ancient parts of the temple go back to the days of Haggai and Zechariah, the high priest Joshua and the Davidic governor, Zerubbabel. That temple, the second temple, was constructed between 520 and 515 B.C. It stood as an ancient symbol of the presence of God for the people of Judah.

The first temple, more grand than the second, had been built under the command of King Solomon to be, as it says in the Book of Kings, a house of prayer for all nations. Empire-builder that he was, Solomon had supposed that Jerusalem would be a world capital and its temple a monument to God's power over all the world. When Solomon's empire failed, the temple became less a universal symbol and more of precious identity to Judah itself. It signaled the presence of God among those people. And when that city was spared in the time of the terrible Assyrian invasions, the temple became even more of a proof of God's abiding protection. "God is in her; she shall not be moved" is what they learned to sing (Psalm 46). Surely

Jerusalem would stand eternal with such a token of God's presence there.

When finally Jerusalem did fall, in the midst of the Babylonian invasions, the hopes of pious Jews were severely damaged. How could such a thing happen? Did it mean, perhaps, that God had abandoned them? Had their story come to an end? But half a century later Babylon's power was broken and they were freed by the decree of the great Persian conqueror, Cyrus. That potentate declared that any Jews who wished might go back to Jerusalem to rebuild from its ruins and construct a new temple. And after some fifteen to twenty years of delay, that is exactly what they did.

That second temple, though humbler than the first, became even more of a sign of God's presence than the first. Now that they were no longer an independent nation but only a district within one of the provinces of the great Persian empire, they had greater need for such a symbol than ever before. The temple had to do for nation and nationhood, king and capital city. The temple became a center for all Jewry. The remnants of the ancient nation would come there over and over as pilgrims. Its base, the knoll named Zion, was like the center of the earth for them. Their psalms reflect their feelings.

> Sing praises to the Lord who dwells in Zion!
> Tell his deeds among his people,
> for he who avenges blood is mindful of them;
> he does not forget the cry of the afflicted.
> *(Psalm 9:11-12)*

In Jesus' day this ancient and crumbling second temple was being surrounded by new structures. The white limestone blocks that rose to prodigious heights as the engineers and builders proceeded were almost incredible in size. Even contemporary visitors coming nineteen and a half centuries later can marvel at what they still see. It was an impressive sight. But Jesus was not impressed. He was saddened. Was it perhaps the old remains that caught his attention more than the modern reconstruction? To a degree, perhaps that was so. But there was also something else that he saw to upset him. To accommodate the needs of pilgrims from afar there were animal merchants and money changers in the courts of the temple. Traveling long distances made it difficult or impossible for many of the pilgrims to bring the lambs or calves or birds required for the sacrifices there. The Judean farmers therefore obliged them with what they could. And to permit the payment of the temple tax in the proper coinage, the money changers offered their services as well. And Jesus was not pleased with all of this.

As we watch, he enters slowly, looking at everything that goes on about him. Then, in a deliberate move, he picks up some cordage and braids himself a whip. He tries it out, moves to the merchants and begins to lash them with it. He kicks over the table of one of the money changers and soon the place is in an uproar.

Sheer bedlam is what we must envision in our minds. On the one side we hear the continued cries of the peddlers: "Lambs, lambs for sale! Buy a kid of the finest quality! Pigeons! Pigeons! A pair of doves is a worthy offering and not so costly as a lamb. Buy my pigeons. The price is low. Why not a chicken? The neck of a chicken will do." Behind us are the sounds of the money changers: "Change your money! You must have the proper money. Coins of the land I give in exchange for any. You come from Tarsus?—from Alexandria, Persia, Rome? It matters not. You can change your currency here." And Jesus moving about in his wrath to silence the cries with the sounds of toppling tables: "Take these things away! You shall not make my Father's house into a house of trade!"

The indignant prophet is what we see. The man from the hills, from Galilee. The pious man of prayer who is offended by the commercialism that has made this all but a house for praying. In moments he is approached by the men who feel themselves in charge of this place. "The Jews" they are called by John but they were only those who had been appointed to represent that people with their own particular politics and piety. "By what authority do you do this?" they cry. "What are your credentials? By what sign do you act? Prove your right to do what you do!"

Jesus' reply is as forceful and deliberate as anything we can imagine. "You are destroying this temple! It is no longer a temple! It is no longer a house of prayer. It has become a place of profit! A place of business! A den of thieves." Then he spreads open his cloak to expose part of his naked torso to say: "But you destroy this temple and I will raise it in three days' time!"

Their response reveals that they took him to be some kind of an eccentric and the fact that they did not understand his gesture. "Young man, do you know how long it has taken to build this temple? Forty-six years! Forty-six years of construction and you will raise it in three days?"

With that we leave this tumultuous scene. We have beheld an important confrontation in which the fate of the temple was in question. To the guardians of that holy place it was the most secure structure in all of creation. As surely as God would abide forever, so would the temple. It had to. To Jesus it was doomed. Its time was done, its end fast approaching. And as the temple would die, so would he. He would be the end for his people and the seed of their new beginning.

Now, after some hours, the scene is different. The noise is no longer about us. We are in a quiet little courtyard somewhere in the same city or somewhere nearby. It is night. The only light is that of the moon and perhaps a flickering lamp or two. As Jesus sits brooding he is approached by a man whose name was Nicodemus. He is one of the Pharisees but one who was quite impressed by what Jesus did with his whip in the temple. He desires to know more about this prophetic man from the territory of Galilee. What follows is a conversation between the two.

"Excuse me, Rabbi. You are alone? Can we talk?" Jesus nods. Nicodemus settles down near him, a bit awkwardly perhaps. "That was quite a demonstration today. The things you said were true. They were right—and good. Such teachings can only come from God. No one could say what you said—do what you did—unless God were with him."

"Amen. Amen, I say, and amen I speak. All that I have to say is simply the truth. And unless a person starts over again he cannot be part of the truth, of the kingdom that is truly God's."

"Unless a person starts over? Like returning to the womb of his mother? How can anything like that be possible?"

"It's true, I tell you. Unless you come from the beginning, from the water and breath of God's creation, you cannot be part of God's realm. What is born by normal means is normal. What is born of the wind is a new breath of God. You must be born from above—born again. Oh, don't be surprised. The wind of creation blows where it wills to blow. You hear it, but you don't really know where it comes from or where it is going. That is what it means to be born of the breath of God. That's how it is for those who are born anew." He was asked about his authority by the men who questioned him in the temple. This, finally, is his answer. It comes from creation, from the very source of his being.

"I don't understand. How can it happen?"

"You are a famous teacher of Israel and you don't understand this? Amen is what I say. The truth. We are speaking of things we understand. We are testifying to what we have seen, but you people don't accept our testimony."

"But Rabbi—that is, I . . . "

"If I speak of ordinary things and you people don't believe, how can you believe if I tell you of extraordinary things? No one has gone up to God's place except the one who comes from God's place: the Son of Man. As Moses, in the wilderness, lifted the primeval serpent from his belly, so the Son of Man must be exalted—in order that all who believe in him shall have enduring life. Whoever believes in that Son of Man shall live."

We can imagine a pause if we will, but Jesus goes on. "God cared enough for the world we live in that he gave his chosen Son, that whoever believes in him should not perish but have life that endures. God did not send the Son into this world to condemn it. To the contrary, he sent the Son to make this world healthy! He who believes in this one is not condemned. But he who does not believe is already condemned by the fact that he does not believe." The judgment is this: light came into our world and people loved darkness more than the light. Why? Because their behavior was evil. All who do evil hate the light. Why? Lest their evil behavior be exposed for what it is. Whoever does what is reliable and true comes into the light that it may be clearly seen that his deeds are being done by God.

We shall allow the scene to fade rather than end. Jesus' words were words of enigma and mystery. At one moment he seems to be talking of general principles that have governed the world from the beginning. At another moment he seems to have been talking about himself. He was finding himself, perhaps, in the very words as he spoke them. In speaking of truth as he did he was describing his own role and destiny. He would live as basic and primeval truth among his people. He would be as a breath from God and that breath would breathe both judgment and life.

Perhaps our own thoughts need to echo his words for ourselves.

> Born from the beginning,
> born of water and wind,
> Child of God, to be what you are,
> you must be born again.
> Born from the beginning,
> born of water and wind.

> Where do you come from,
> you who appear in our temple?
> You who upset the tables of change,
> driving us out of our sacred courts?
> You speak like a prophet, son of man,
> but where do you come from?
> What is your sign?

> Born from the beginning,
> born of water and wind.
> Child of God, to be what you are,
> you must be born again.
> Born from the beginning,
> born of water and wind.

Three

The Sign of the Well

Jerusalem was not the only holy city in the era of the old covenant. While the kingdom of Judah, the kingdom of the south and of David, celebrated Jerusalem and Mount Zion, the northern kingdom, which called itself Israel, had temples at both Bethel and Dan.

The northern kingdom fell to the Assyrian invasion in the eighth century B.C. One hundred and fifty years before Jerusalem was destroyed by the Babylonian invaders, both Bethel and Dan bit the dust and the citizens of Israel suffered exile and occupation.

While Jews came back to rebuild Jerusalem, remnants of ancient Israel reclaimed themselves as the province of Samaria. They too wanted a temple for God. They even volunteered to help with the rebuilding of Jerusalem's temple but the Jews rejected their offer on the grounds that the Samaritans were a people of mixed blood and impure religion.

Not to be utterly dissuaded by that or outdone by their southern rivals, the Samaritans built themselves a temple on the top of Mount Gerizim where the laws of Moses had once been proclaimed by Joshua. It became their religious rallying point and a convincing rival to the temple in Jerusalem. Mount Gerizim was clearly higher than the knoll called Mount Zion, where Jerusalem's temple stood. And with a tradition that went back to Joshua and the patriarch Jacob it claimed greater antiquity than David's royal city.

In one of the many squabbles between Jews and Samaritans, a regiment or more of Jewish soldiers went north and destroyed the Samaritan temple on Mount Gerizim. That was during the time of the Maccabees when Jews ruled Samaria and other districts of the area and enjoyed some independence from their Syrian masters. That was a hundred years before the birth of Jesus. It was the last of many foul deeds that created bad blood between these two groups who shared a common ancestry.

And now that we are reminded of all these matters, let us follow Jesus as he journeyed through Samaritan country.

We are at the foot of Mount Gerizim, looking at the ancient well that was supposedly dug by the patriarch Jacob himself. The thought of the cool water in its depths tempts the thirst of the man who pauses there, but nothing can be done to relieve the temptation. The well is deep. There is nothing at hand for the drawing of water. The thought of food follows the thought of water. The companions of Jesus decide to walk to the nearby Samaritan village of Sychar to find something to eat. Perhaps even a drink of water for their thirst.

It is with a bit of uncertainty and trepidation that they walk over to that village. They are Jews in alien territory. The Samaritan villagers might refuse them on those grounds alone. There was every reason for Samaritans to mistrust these Jews.

Jesus decides to stay by the well while his friends go into the village. Does the place intrigue him? Or is it the thought of the cool well water that keeps him there? While he sits there a woman approaches from the very village to which his disciples have gone for food. He watches her. She tries hard not to notice him. In the way that she has done it thousands of times before, in the way that countless women had done it millions of times before, she draws water from Jacob's well. At this point Jesus speaks.

"Give me a drink if you will, please."

"How is it that you, a Jew, ask a Samaritan woman for a drink of water?"

"If you knew it was God's gift and all that God has to give—and who it is that is asking you—you would have asked him and he would have given you flowing water of life."

"Mister, you have nothing to draw the water with and this well is deep. Where would you get your flowing water? Are you smarter than our ancestor Jacob who gave us this well and drank from it himself—he and his sons and his cattle?"

"Whoever drinks this water will get thirsty again. Is that not right? Whoever drinks of the water I can give will never get thirsty again. The water I give will become a spring within that wells up to provide enduring life."

At this remark the woman becomes a bit sarcastic. "Well, then, give me this water, sir—that I may not thirst or ever have to come back here for more."

"Go get your husband and bring him here."

She is stunned by this remark, for it reveals more than the truth about herself. It represents the attitude that all Jews held toward Samaritans, for the Jews regarded the old kingdom of Israel and its descendants as a troupe of adulterers. Hosea, the single prophetic book from the old northern kingdom, had characterized his people in just that manner and Jews heartily agreed with his characterization. This is an ancient insult that could be spoken only by a Jew and only by one who knew the Samaritan past.

"You sound like a prophet," says the woman. Does she have knowledge of her own people's prophet, Hosea? "Our fathers worshiped on this mountain, sir." She gestures toward Mount Gerizim. "You Jews say that Jerusalem is the place where men ought to worship."

"Woman, believe me: the time is coming when you will worship the Father neither on this mountain nor in Jerusalem." The words come from one who had already foreseen the fall of the Jewish holy city. Forty years hence his premonition would be verified. "You worship in your ignorance. We worship in the knowledge that salvation comes from the Jews." (Did he have to say that?) "The hour is coming—it is already here—when those who truly worship the Father will worship in the manner of the wind and in truth. God is the breath of creation. Those who worship him must worship in the manner of the wind and in truth."

"I know the Anointed One is coming. When he comes, will he teach us these things?" She was a true Samaritan in her expectations, for the Samaritans awaited an anointed teacher rather than an anointed king, a new Moses rather than a new David.

"He speaks to you now," says Jesus. And then the dialogue is interrupted. Jesus' companions appear, returning from the village with food. The woman is a bit nonplussed by this. She soon leaves and heads toward the village. The disciples have noticed her, of course. A couple of them cast knowing glances while the rest try to ignore her. They switch their attention to the food they have brought. "Rabbi, we must eat," they say. "Here. We have brought food."

"I have been eating of food that you missed." They are puzzled and once again look in the direction of the woman who left the scene. "Did she bring him food while we were away?" mutters one. "What went on while we were gone?" asks another. Jesus ignores their comments and continues, "To do the desire of the One who sent me, that is my food. I must accomplish his work." Then he looks out over the lush plain that lies to the east of Mount Gerizim. "You see the valley before you? You see the grain fields? 'Four months more and then the harvest,' that's what you say. I tell you, if you *lift* your eyes you will see that the fields are already ripe for harvest. Yes, I have had food to eat. Whoever reaps will be fed.

He will gather produce for life that endures. Sower and harvester, they shall be happy together.

"There is another true saying you have: 'One sows, another reaps.' I sent you to the village as harvesters, to gather what others have labored for. They put in their labor to produce the bread you eat." He gestures to indicate their hearty eating. "You now join in their efforts."

At this point we are interrupted by the sounds of approaching people. Our Samaritan woman has been to the village to summon her neighbors and a sizable group is coming with her. We hear her speaking to them as they come.

"I tell you, he told me the truth about me and the truth about all of us. The truth of our prophet. He knows our story. He is the Teacher we wait for." But now that she has brought them close enough to converse with Jesus we can imagine them speaking as follows. "Rabbi, welcome! This woman has told us about you and we would like to hear more of what you have to say. We have room in our homes for you—for all of you. Come, do come, and stay with us for a while."

This is the climax of the sign, for now we behold the true miracle: Samaritans welcoming Jews and Jews acting as brothers to Samaritans. The world had waited several centuries for this. Ezekiel the prophet had dared to predict it. Other prophets had repeated this hope. Now it was coming to fulfillment.

"The hour is coming," said Jesus, "when those who truly worship the Father will worship in the manner of the wind and in truth." In the little scroll of Malachi we find this line: "Have we not all one Father? Did not one God create us?" That too was about proper worship. As the Wind, the Breath, the Spirit of God—they are all one word in the biblical tongue—embrace all and inspire all of creation, so Jesus saw that Spirit of God embracing both Jew and Samaritan. It was the miracle of reconciliation. Later in their lives his disciples would see even greater signs as the message went out to reconcile yet more peoples and become a universal movement. For now this was but a sign. But if Samaritan and Jew could be as one family, why not all the world? If that ancient enmity could be ended so cheerfully as this, why not all enmity in the same way?

This was a taste of resurrection: the resurrection of human fellowship that had through its own folly died. Jesus had moved into the middle, challenged the issue with sharp and perceptive words, but through the pain of that challenge he had brought about the miracle of reconciliation.

Let us imagine some closing lines to finish our little drama. Let us imagine Jesus' disciples saying such things as the following.

"Samaritans inviting us to their homes? Who would have dreamed of such a day?"

"Dare we go with them, or is it a trick?"

"Come, let's go with them. Perhaps they have more good food to share. Their food is good."

And imagine the Samaritans responding with this.

"Why not? What is a Samaritan? What is a Jew? Are we not all children of God? And does not the Anointed One come for us all?"

Many more came to believe, we read in the text of John's Gospel, and in the Book of Acts we learn that the evangel of Jesus succeeded with many in Samaria.

Four

The Sign of the Healer

Today we journey to a village of ancient Galilee. It is the village of Cana, where we recently beheld Jesus at a wedding feast. As villages go it is not distinctive. There is the little market square, near the entrance of the country road, where the old men gather every day. There are the usual stone houses. One is built against another to produce a maze of alleys in which a stranger could easily get lost even though the village is not that large a place. The people who live here are people who make their living from the soil and the various craftsmen who serve the business of farmers.

Other people come through from time to time. Among them are members of the Roman occupation force. The country was under the rule of the Roman legions, we must remember, and that brought soldiers from distant lands for duty in this place. It is the appearance of a Roman officer, in fact, that sets off the drama of this scene.

"Rabbi! Rabbi, pardon my intrusion, but I must request of you something. They say that you heal—with a touch, with a word. Is it true? My son, my own dear son, is desperately ill. The fever has not left him for days and now it becomes worse."

"Unless you see signs and wonders you will not believe?"

"No, no, it's not that at all! I am not merely curious about you. It's my son! He is ill and I fear for his life. Come down, sir, and help me before he dies!"

We have imagined the speech of the Roman officer, of course, for they are not recorded in John's brief account. But they had to be something like this, for this was clearly a desperate man willing to go to any length in order to save the life of his son. And for a Roman officer to approach a Jewish healer was not easy. It is clear that Jesus discerned all this. His response was simple and convincing.

"You may return to your home without fear. Your son will live."

The man was apparently wordless. But he must have believed or at least deeply desired to believe what Jesus said. He turned and left for Capernaum. On his way home he was met by friends who greeted him with the good news that his son was alive and healing. And the father, says John, realized that the fever had subsided at the time when Jesus spoke the reassuring words.

"This was the second sign given by Jesus on his way from Judea to Galilee," we read in the Gospel. But it also serves as a prelude to a fuller sign that took place in Jerusalem itself and immediately follows this one in the text. So we must move our minds back to this world capital of all Jewry, in Jesus' time as now. We are in a certain section of that city wherein we find a large pool of water. Because its waters are reputed to have a healing effect whenever the spring beneath bubbles a bit, a sizable group of invalids are gathered around, each waiting for the magic moment when he or she might be healed. This is the famed pool of Bethzatha. Those gathered have come to it from afar in hope or desperation. To help set the scene prior to the action that most concerns us, let us imagine a conversation that expresses the awareness of those who were really there.

"See that poor fellow there? He has been waiting nearly forty years and never made it yet."

"They say that when the water stirs, the first person to get into the pool will be healed."

"Some say an angel moves the water."

In the midst of this kind of observation, Jesus approaches the one of whom they were speaking—an invalid of thirty-eight years who is apparently extremely helpless. Jesus addresses him with this interesting question: "Do you want to be healed?"

"Mister, I have no one to put me into the pool when the water is troubled." With his eyes he indicates his wretched condition. "When I am trying to get to the pool another always steps down before me."

"Get up. Pick up your sleeping mat and try walking."

The man is virtually stunned by the command. When he obeys it is perhaps because of the very authority with which the words were spoken. But he has not walked for a very long time and therefore every move is a new experiment. We need to imagine a procedure in which each movement is a new discovery. It is as though we are watching a primeval Adam trying his limbs for the very first time. For this man it is like going back to the beginning, like being born out of the original clay and experiencing that first breath of life that was breathed into man by the Creator. This is new birth being acted out before us. It is like the birth of a baby in which one watches to see if the suckling will make it except that the subject is a crippled, grown man.

When the man finally discovered that he could, indeed, walk his whole personality must have given way to incredible joy. And those gathered around must have been thoroughly amazed. Here was such a healing as would fulfill all the dreams and desires of any modern TV evangelist. It was a spectacular show. But as we look around for the one who seems to have inspired it, we do not find him. Jesus has disappeared from the scene. The man with the mat is left to himself. But never mind, he must complete his orders. He had been told to pick up his mat and carry it away, so he commences to do that. But not for long. The guardians of the sabbath are there and this is a sabbath day. No burdens are to be borne on the day of rest.

"Halt!" they cry. "It is the sabbath. You desecrate the sabbath by carrying your bedclothes. You must not work on the sabbath!"

How should the man respond? The fact that this was the first time in thirty-eight years when he actually could perform such a deed had filled him with uncontainable joy. Now they dashed cold water on his delight with their reprimands. And yet, just think of it, he was finally capable of actually sinning! But he replies simply. "The fellow who healed me—he told me, 'Pick up your sleeping mat and try walking.'"

"Fool! Who is this fellow who told you"—and perhaps the next words are in mimic of his own voice—"'Pick up your sleeping mat and try walking'?"

"I–I–I don't know." He looks about in confusion. "I don't know...." The poor fellow wanders off, looking about him this way and that to catch sight of Jesus. He drops his mat when he sees that critics are still watching. We follow him as he makes his way to the temple, no doubt to have himself declared clean and whole by the priests. There he finally encounters the man who healed him. Jesus speaks before he can. "Look! You are well. Now don't get into any more trouble or something worse might happen to you."

As Jesus moves away the man runs back to the sabbath guardians, pointing excitedly toward Jesus to identify his benefactor for them. They approach and make their way all the way to the one who is pointed out. Jesus senses their coming and turns to address them. "My Father works on the sabbath," he says. "Therefore I work on the sabbath. My Father gives life on the sabbath as well as on any other day of the week.

Therefore I give life on the sabbath." His opponents stiffen, offended by his remarks. They mutter subdued comments but Jesus goes on. "The Son cannot act without the Father's permission, can he? How can God give permission to heal on the sabbath? The Son only does what he sees the Father doing. But the Father loves the Son and therefore he shows him all that he does.

"Don't wonder over this. You will see greater things. The Father gives life; therefore the Son gives life. The Father raises the dead and so shall the Son." His words cause increasing consternation. Their expressions change to suggest that they have evil intent for this brash healer. "The Father leaves the judging to the Son," he continues, "where to do this and when to do that. Therefore the Son has his honor." With these words he likely gestured toward the people around him, for he may have meant all of God's sons as much as himself and perhaps most particularly the man who had just learned to walk and therefore deserved some congratulations and honor. "If you do not honor the Son, you are dishonoring the Father."

The response must have been electric. Questions must have arisen and come to expression. "What does he mean?" "Does he refer to the fellow who was healed or is he talking about himself?" "Does he think himself equal to God?"

Jesus' voice raises to address the crowd gathering around. "Amen, amen! I tell you the truth! The hour is coming, the hour is here! The dead hear the voice of the Son of God and those who hear will live! As the Father has life, so he gives life to the Son—and the authority to judge for himself because he is the Son of Man." Now he lowers his voice a bit to speak more directly to those who were arguing with him. "Don't act so surprised. You have spoken like this yourselves. Even you have said it: the hour is coming when all who are in the tombs shall hear his voice. And they will come forth—those who have done good to the resurrection of life, those who have done evil to the resurrection of judgment."

"He goes too far." "What does he mean?" "His words could be blasphemy. He assumed to know the secrets of God." So we might imagine the comments that represent the mood and thoughts of his opponents on that occasion according to John.

"I do nothing on my own authority," said Jesus. "I judge as I have been told to judge. My judgment is just, only because I do not seek my own will. I do only the will of him who sent me." To this there had to be strong reaction. They move in on him but some of the people rise to defend him. He continues after the unrest is contained.

"I understand. Every man needs a witness. He cannot witness to himself, right? It says so in the torah. There must be at least two witnesses. Well, I have three. The first? John. John, who baptized by the Jordan. Surely you must remember him. He was a burning and shining light. You rejoiced in that light—for a while. Do you remember how he spoke of one who was coming? Of one whose sandals he could not unlatch? He was my first witness. My works also bear witness. They are the works of God, for they are works that give life." They rise to object. He motions them to desist and concedes, with a mocking mime to their objection.

"My third witness is the torah. Yes, Moses himself. He wrote about me because he wrote about the things that I do. About healing and loving your neighbor as yourself. 'And God called to Moses'—the Book of Leviticus, right? But if you do not believe the writings of Moses, how will you ever believe me? So believe only in the life-giving works."

We must now imagine Jesus walking away, leaving the guardians of the sabbath in a burning rage. But there must have been many who showed their approval. The crowd must have been divided or we would not know what we know.

As we construct dialogue and drama out of what is a long soliloquy in the Gospel text we gain the impression that Jesus became more and more forcefully what he came to be. At this point we see him as one who understood his task to be that of bringing life and health into a society that was sick and dying. In that task he could only be representing God because only God can give life or perform healing. That was his chief endorsement for what he was doing. And that was a fulfillment of the very torah that his Jewish opponents espoused most dearly. The sabbath could hardly be dishonored by such deeds!

To such a man one might sing the traditional greeting of sabbath with special meaning.

>Come, Beloved, to meet the Bride,
>to greet and receive the sabbath!

And to sabbath herself one might continue,

>Enter in peace, enter in joy!
>Enter rejoicing in the midst of your faithful and
>   precious people.
>Enter, O Bride, O Bride of the Lord!

The sabbath was for rejoicing. Jesus saw himself as one who should make it possible for all to rejoice. He sought to bring joy through the restoration of life. He labored that life might arise anew wherever it had been thwarted or put down.

Five

The Sign of the Bread

Imagine ourselves on a hillside—a rocky hillside, for all the hillsides of ancient Galilee were rocky, but with green growth of spring overcrowding the rocks. We are not alone. Thousands of people are gathering with us. Were it not for the first century Galilean costumery and the lack of blaring amplifiers we might think ourselves at an open-air rock concert.

Our hillside overlooks a lake that is known in our tradition as the Sea of Galilee. The natives call it Kinnereth and it is not a sea at all but a fresh-water lake.

We who are here have come from the villages around to listen to one who calls himself the Son of Man. We have taken him to be a prophet because his words seem to be gifts of God. We desire to hear what he has to say. We have come to feast on whatever words he may speak today.

If we can stand a bit of contemporary intrusion into the scene we have now imagined, let us have piped in the soft sounds of a hymn of Holy Communion. The traditional "O Bread of Life from Heaven" would be ideal. Anything that will suggest that this is a colossal Communion service and that we who have gathered are gathering for somewhat the same reason that people gather to commune in the Lord's Supper in our time. And let the thought of bread, a key line of that hymn, tantalize our hunger. It is bread we would like. We are hungry.

But now let us speed our imaginations. Jesus speaks for a long time but we shall compress all that into a single sermon of length and let us pretend that the sermon is over. Because John, the author of the Gospel text, chose to omit the sermon, we must also do that and get to the sign that most mattered. So the sermon is over, we are hungry, and Jesus has noticed our hunger. We know that from the comment he makes at the end of his discourse. As he looks at the crowd he says to his disciples, "Where can we find some bread for these people to eat?"

One named Philip replies. "Two hundred days' wages would not buy enough for each of them to get even a little."

Another, named Andrew, speaks a second response. "I saw a lad here with five barley loaves and two fish. That wouldn't go far with a crowd like this, though, would it?"

"Tell the people to sit," says Jesus. The disciples are now accustomed to surprises on the part of this strange friend they follow. They dutifully obey. And because the crowd is large we can imagine that to carry out his command required a good bit of shouting and commotion. Finally, when they have succeeded, Jesus says, "Bring the lad with the fish." So Andrew presents the boy he had seen. The boy stands there. Jesus takes the loaves from him in a gentle manner. He holds one aloft and breaks it, perhaps pronouncing the traditional blessing of bread as he does it. Then the bread is distributed as he passes it on to his companions and they pass it on to the people in the crowd. But lo, the miracle! As the bread is passed from one to another it seems to multiply in the hands. And the same with the fish, which is dealt with in a similar manner. The bread and the fish are multiplying to serve the hunger of thousands.

Now, lest we be caught up in the miracle itself, we must be reminded of the significance of bread and fish. The bread of Holy Communion, of course, is familiar to us. Fish was a

The Sign of the Bread

similar food to the early followers. A fish would become the symbol of early Christian communities. The very word that signified the fish in the language of the Greeks would come to signify the early Christian credo as well. Fish was special.

As the food is distributed and eaten we hear increasing murmurs of satisfaction. And if we are still tuned into the music of "O Bread of Life," the suggestion of our Great Supper should be in mind. Then the satisfied sounds give way to voices that actually speak clear lines.

"If this man were our ruler there would be plenty and peace."

"Would that this one were our king."

"A man like this would be better than living under Caesar. Caesar promises but does not fulfill. This man delivers from the start."

There is Messiah talk in the air and the crowd is becoming restless with it. They begin to press upon Jesus. They are ominous. They are a mass that could quickly become the core of a political uprising. Jesus retreats. With the help of his friends he makes his way to the hills, to the ravines of the bluffs that tower above the lake. In a short time he has disappeared and the mob mills about in confusion.

That evening the disciples went down to the shore of the lake, we read in the Gospel of John. They got into a boat to make for the other side of the lake, to the village that was called Capernaum. They sailed without him, but as they approached the rocky shore they saw him walking. Illusory or real, it appeared to them that he was walking on the surface of the water. "Look! He walks on the water!" one cries. But we are so suddenly at the shore that we cannot be sure. "Do not be afraid. It is I," responds Jesus, and this stills their alarm. He sits with them and we, with them, enjoy the relief of some moments of privacy. But it is interrupted all too soon. The crowd from the other side of the lake has followed around the shore and they are upon us, pressing with enthusiastic political desires.

Jesus rises to address them. "Why are you following me?" he says. "Is it because of the signs I give? No, surely not. It is because you have eaten your fill of the bread. You should not be anxious for perishable bread but for food that endures. You should desire the food that is given by the Son of Man who knows God as Father."

As the people respond to this we cannot help but note their willingness to learn from him. "What kind of work shall we do to please God?" they say. Work they understand. They know how to work. These are working people and they are willing to please with their work if we but show them what to do. Jesus could have had them in the palm of his hands, so willing they were. Perhaps he did.

"This is the work of God: have faith in him whom God sends."

They clamor to reply to his words. "Are you the one he has sent?" "By what sign shall we know that we should believe in you, if not for the bread?" "What else can you do? You gave us bread. Our fathers got bread in the wilderness too—bread from heaven, the bread called manna."

"You know, do you not," says Jesus, "that it was not Moses who gave the manna. It was God. And it is my Father who even now gives you the true bread from heaven."

A single voice speaks from the crowd: "Give us that bread forever, sir."

"I, myself, am the bread. The only bread that I have to give is myself. But whoever comes to me will not go hungry again. Whoever believes in me shall not thirst. Yet it is as I told you: you can see me and still not believe. Whoever sees and believes shall have enduring life. On the final day I shall raise him."

The Sign of the Bread

The people turn to converse with each other. "'I am the bread from heaven,' he says. Yet we know his father and mother in Nazareth. How can he say that he comes from heaven?"

"No one comes to me unless the Father draws him to me. It is written in the prophets: 'They will all be taught by God.' To hear that teaching of the Father and learn it is to come to me. No one has seen the Father. Only he who has come from God knows God. But everyone who believes has life that endures.

"I am bread. I am the life-giving bread." He picks up a piece of bread in his hand and holds it. He studies it for a moment. "Your fathers ate the manna in the wilderness and they are dead." He lets the piece of bread fall to the ground. He looks up to the eyes of those who listen, being simply himself as he continues to speak. "This bread comes from heaven so that people may eat and not die. Whoever eats this bread shall live on." He begins to walk about in an agitated manner. "The bread I give for the life of the world is my flesh."

Suddenly there is an outburst from one of Jesus' companions. "This is intolerable language! How could anyone accept it?" That man and a few others depart. Jesus calls after them. "Does this upset you? What if you should see the Son of Man ascend to where he was?" He turns to address those who are still with him. "It is the breath of God that gives life. The flesh has nothing to offer. The words that I have spoken to you—they are breath and they are life."

Do we understand? Do we understand what he meant? The play on such terms as "words" and "breath" in juxtaposition to the bread and the fish is a way of turning our attention from simple to profound understanding of what he was saying. The multiplying of bread and fish suggested the obvious: here was a savior who could provide. He could give the basics of life. Yet he desired to give more than this. He desired to give himself, to give all that he was and could be. He desired that his people have life and so he was willing to give the totality of his existence, which was all the life that was in his hands. They would have to receive him in order to truly take life in its fullness. Only in taking him could they have it all.

Therefore he spoke of himself as the truest bread that he had to give. To have that bread they would have to listen to him, receive him on whatever terms he might choose to come to them. They would have to believe in him as the Son of Man that he was.

Six

The Sign of Sight

Once again we go to the city of Jerusalem. We are in a public square, a place where human traffic flows. By the side of the street we see a blind beggar. Everyone in this place knows that he has been blind from birth. Even Jesus' companions know it. Yet he is only one of many who sit here to beg. This is, after all, the Holy City. Those who come here are pilgrims, and pilgrims are prone to give alms to the poor. So here the beggars assemble to prevail upon the sympathies of whoever will practice mercy.

This is a small reward for what the blind and the maimed and the ill have to put up with from the culture at large, for that was a time and place when and where people generally thought that folks who suffer misfortune were folks being punished by God. There was a notion that God rather consistently rewards the good for their goodness and punishes the wicked. And to judge the matter seemed simple: people who enjoyed good fortune were people being rewarded by God while those who suffered misfortune were being penalized for their sins. Jesus' own disciples had been brought up to think that way. What we hear them say as they encounter the blind man betrays what they think.

"Rabbi, who sinned that he was born blind? Is this a punishment for his own sin or the sin of his parents?"

Jesus immediately corrects their thinking. "Do you really think such things are so? Neither he nor his parents sinned. This is the work of God. He is blind so that we might see the work of God." He raises his voice for whoever might be gathering around. "As long as daylight lasts I must do the work of the One who sent me. The night is coming when no one can work. I must be the light of this world as long as I am in it." Then the great rabbi does something that would seem puzzling to any of us. He stooped, spat into the dust and made mud with his saliva. Then he put that mud like a plaster over the man's eyes and said, "Go and wash your eyes in the Pool of Siloam."

Surely Jesus' companions must have had to help the blind man away to the pool. Let us imagine them doing that—and hearing the sounds of surprise and delight as the man washed his eyes and received his sight. It was an astounding thing, a wonder beyond his hope. Who could contain the feelings that would ensue? There must have been cries of surprise and a general hubbub of excitement. Yet dominating all other sounds we must hear the man crying aloud, "I can see! I can see! Praise the Lord, I can see!"

In response to this there were several reactions on the part of those who had become accustomed to the sight of this blind beggar in this particular part of the city. "Who is this?" "Is this the man who used to sit here and beg?" "Yes, it is." "No, it is not. He only looks a bit like him."

The last remark is the cue line for our beggar. "I am! I am that man!"

"How is it that you see?" ask those who had not been present but came running at the sound of excitement. "How did you get your sight?" One gets the impression that Jerusalem harbored many who loved miracles.

"The man they call Jesus did it. He made a paste and put it on my eyes and said to me, 'Go, wash in the Pool of Siloam.' I did it. I went, I washed, and now I can see! Isn't it wonderful?"

"Where is he—this Jesus who did it?"

The Sign of Sight

The man looks around, but in vain. Jesus has disappeared. Apparently he had a habit of disappearing at moments like this. The man stammers a response. "He ... I ... I don't know. Where did he go?"

But suddenly the gathering crowd of people has another concern. "We should take him to the Pharisees." "They would be interested in this. They tell us such miracles can happen and now one has. They will surely want to know about it." "Come with us," say some to the man who has received his sight and they lead him away to the men whom we have before known as the guardians of the sabbath.

"So," say the sabbath guardians, "what is this all about?"

"This man was blind until today. But suddenly he can see. The fellow called Jesus gave him his sight."

"Really? Well, tell us how this happened. Give us your account, beggar man."

The man answers simply. "He put clay on my eyes and I washed and now I can see."

The responses to this are multiple. "That's all there was to it? Surely he must have done more than that." "By what authority did he do this deed? He is not authorized by God, for he does not even keep the sabbath. Making mortar on the sabbath is forbidden." And, in a more sympathetic vein we hear, "Well, if this really did occur, how can we say that it—that he, that is—is not authorized by God? Surely a sinner cannot perform such a sign." The group is divided in its opinion as any good group of Jewish men would be. One turns to the man and says, "What do you say about him, since it was your eyes that were healed?"

"He is a prophet."

There is a general stir of surprise and some disapproval.

"Call this man's parents. Someone bring his parents here." But the parents are already approaching, for someone had gone to tell them what had occurred. They came bewildered and amazed. And fearful at seeing an assembly of Pharisees, for such men have labeled them sinners because they brought a blind child into the world. They tremble as they are addressed. "Is this your son whom they say was born blind? Do you know him? How is it that he now sees?"

"Yes, yes, he is our son," says the mother. "And he was born blind." At this she breaks down and weeps. "But this," continues the father, "this is a mystery to us, this fact that he sees. We only heard of it now. We do not know how it happened." The man pauses to offer some comfort to his wife and to look at the joyful face of his son. Then he turns again to the Pharisees and says, "He is of age. Ask him how it happened. Let him speak for himself. As for us, we had nothing to do with this—this miracle." And so all attention is turned to the son who is now addressed by the Pharisees. "We bind you by oath to tell the truth and nothing but the truth. Give God the glory."

"To God be all glory!" shouts the son with enthusiastic joy.

"This man who gave you your sight—he is not a good man. He violates the sabbath." Their tone is condescending as well as judgmental.

"Good man or bad man I do not know. I only know this: I was blind but now I see."

"How did he do it? What did he do to you? How did he open your eyes?"

"I already told you and you would not listen. Why do you want to hear it again? Do you, too, want to be his disciples?" They react with a sudden shock of anger.

"*You* may be his disciple. *We* are disciples of Moses. We know that God spoke to Moses. As for this man, we don't even know where he comes from."

"How strange! How extraordinary! You don't know where he comes from, yet he opened my eyes. You have taught us

The Sign of Sight

that God does not listen to sinners or answer the prayers of the wicked—that God only listens to good men. Never since the world began has it happened that a person born blind was given his sight. If this man were not from God he could not do such a thing!"

"You were born in sin and your blindness is proof of it—the very penalty and proof of your guilt! Who are you to teach us?"

Then those authoritative leaders of men moved to expel both him and his parents from the scene. They are to be cast out as sinners lest they contaminate the health of the whole. "Be off with you and learn of repentance!" they cry.

Now the man wanders off by himself and is soon met by Jesus, who encounters him with pleasure. "Do you believe in the Son of Man?" asks Jesus. "Do you believe in what is destined for us who are human?"

"Who is that Son of Man, sir, that I might believe in him?"

"The Son of Man, the true human—that is the man you first saw and the man who now speaks to you."

"Indeed, sir? I believe. Yes, I believe."

And Jesus raises his voice that others might hear his words as he continues to speak. "For judgment I came, that those who do not see may see and that those who see may be blind."

The guardians of the sabbath, who have wandered this way, hear his words. They call out with defiance, "Do you mean to insinuate that we are blind?"

"Blind?" shouts Jesus. "If you were blind you would have no guilt. But because you claim to see, your guilt remains."

This, of course, is the line that should arrest us. This is the crux of the sign. There were those who thought they lived in the light, who thought they understood reality, who thought themselves wise enough to lead the blind. But suddenly the tables are turned. All their presumed knowledge now appears to be sinful presumption. Those who thought themselves righteous are now declared to be sinners. And the man who had been labeled a sinner by them is now the one who truly understands. Not that he understood much but he did understand what was most essential. He knew that sight is a gift and a miracle. He knew that it comes from God and was not a matter of mortal achievement. He understood the grace by which we are all sustained and redeemed.

The drama proceeds a bit further. Jesus has begun to think more thoughts about these self-appointed leaders of the blind who are obviously more blind than those whom they pretend to lead. They were dangerous men who needed to be challenged. He speaks his mind to disciples gathered around him.

"There are shepherds who are not true shepherds. They are thieves and robbers. They shepherd for the sake of their own honor but not for the sake of the sheep. How do you know the thief? He does not enter through the gate. He climbs over the fence to get at the sheep. But the true shepherd—ah, he knows the sheep. He comes to the gate and calls them by name and each sheep comes, for they know the true shepherd's voice. The sheep will not listen to a stranger. They run at the sound of the stranger's voice."

His thoughts turn to himself. He cannot criticize and not consider whether he has the right to usurp their role. "Am I a shepherd? I am only the gate. I see the sheep and I see the shepherds. Yet I know the sheep and so, in a way, I am the true shepherd. I know who are mine and they know me."

Yet not far away a group of his enemies gather in a huddle to discuss his words and his ways. "This man is possessed by a demon. He is mad! We should not so much as listen to him." "But his words are not the words of a madman. And what demon can open the eyes of the blind?" "Are you taken

The Sign of Sight

in by that? It was only a trick! It cannot be real." They are not in agreement and yet they are agreed to confront him. They break into his circle with one bold question: "You keep us in suspense too long. If you mean to be the Messiah, why don't you tell us plainly?"

"I told you what I can tell you but you would not believe. It is my works alone that bear witness to what I am. But I know why you do not believe: you are not my sheep. My sheep hear my voice. I know them by name and they follow me. None of them shall ever perish and no one shall ever snatch them from my hand." His speech increases in intensity. "My Father, who gave them to me, is greater than all. And no one is able to snatch them out of my hand. I and my Father are one."

"That is blasphemy! You and the Father are one! Indeed! For that you deserve to be stoned!"

"The works that I do are my Father's works. Is it for that you would stone me? The father lives on in the son according to our tradition. If I do not do the works of the Father, then I am not his Son and you should not believe me. But if I do the works of my Father . . . " With this they try to lay hands upon him, to arrest him, but he escapes. They were about to stone him, it says in the Gospel text, but he hid himself and left the temple. Surely things were moving toward the inevitable sacrifice. The more he did to represent life and light, the more surely did he move toward death and darkness.

Seven

The Sign of the Tomb

As Jesus proceeded on his journey toward resurrection it became ever more clearly a journey through death. In seeking to bring life and light into the world that surrounded him he became ever more aware of its death and darkness. He had asserted the joy of the wedding. He had asserted healing. He had asserted the truth of devotion to God, the truth of bread and water and sight. Ultimately he would have to face the truth about death and assert life itself within that harsh context.

Along the way he spoke of the necessity of dying. He had begun to realize that he, like a grain of wheat, would have to be buried in order to bear his fruit. But how could it happen? How can life come out of dying? The seventh sign would be a proof of that.

Imagine, if you will, a rock-cut tomb, one of a series of tombs on the edge of a hill. Each tomb is a cave with multiple chambers. If it matters, the place is Bethany, just east of the Holy City. To the east the land drops away to Jericho, down in the Jordan Valley. To the west and the north and the south the hills continue.

We are among the tombs. Better still, we are within one of them. In the back chamber, if you please, having to squint as we look toward the light that comes as a shaft through the slightly arched opening. For the sake of best understanding this episode of our drama we need to imagine ourselves among the dead.

The Sign of the Tomb

We hear voices. The first is that of Martha, one of the dear friends of Jesus who lives here in Bethany. She is speaking to a public messenger, directing him to bear a message to her esteemed friend. Her brother Lazarus is ill. She fears that he may die.

"You tell him simply this: he whom you love is ill. He will know who it is."

"Have no fear, good woman. I shall be there soon. Within the day or by morning tomorrow."

Together with Martha, Mary her sister bids the messenger farewell on his journey. Then each turns to the other with tears of anxiety as Mary cries out, "Oh, if Lazarus dies, if Lazarus dies! This is the one he loved so much, our brother who seems so close to departing."

With that we must allow our minds to travel with the messenger. Some distance away from these tombs the messenger eventually reaches his destination to say, "I have a message for you, sir: he whom you love is ill. It is from Martha of Bethany. That is all I was told to say."

"Thank you. Thank you, my good man. Judas, give him a messenger's pay."

Judas obeys, but he and the others are alarmed at the news upset that Jesus responds with no apparent alarm on his part. "It must be serious, Rabbi," says one. "Martha and Mary would not send such a message unless it were serious. They are hoping that we will come and that you will heal him."

"The illness is not fatal. It is to God's glory. God will be glorified by it."

Was he so much the prophet that he even foresaw what would happen? The Gospel writer seems to have thought so. Or was he biding time to discover for himself what the Father's will might be? Perhaps he sensed some kind of a test that demanded both patience and obedience on his part. Whatever be the reason, that we cannot know. Only two days later did he declare, "It is time to go to Judea again." By that time another concern caused the disciples to retort, "Rabbi, the authorities were seeking to stone you there. Why go again?"

"There are twelve hours of daylight. Whoever walks in the daylight does not stumble. He sees the light of this world. Only those who walk in the night will stumble," and he chuckles as he adds: "That is because there is no light in them! Our friend Lazarus has fallen asleep. I go to Judea to awaken Lazarus out of his sleep."

"If he is but sleeping, Rabbi, he will recover."

"Lazarus is dead. And for your sakes I am glad that I wasn't there, so that you may believe. But let us go to him."

The response can only have been somewhat cynical or sarcastic. "Let's all go then, so that we may die with him."

But now let us transport our minds back to the tombs so that we may experience what is happening as Jesus journeys into Judea. A shrouded body is being carried into the very tomb where we have positioned ourselves. We, who are now among the dead, are being joined by one of our brothers. Lazarus has died and we are receiving his body into the tomb. Behind him, outside the tomb, are his two sisters, Martha and Mary, and others of family and friends who have gathered in grief. It is a familiar scene, for death is a familiar experience in this world of ours. We are beholding a funeral but as those from beyond rather than one of the grievers.

Three days after this is the day that Jesus arrives with his companions. He is met by Martha. "My Lord, Lord Jesus!" she cries. "If you had been here he would not have died!" Her tears swallow her words for a moment before she continues, "But even now, Lord, I know that whatever you ask from God, God will grant you."

"Your brother will rise."

The Sign of the Tomb

"Oh, I know that. I know that. I know that he will rise again on the final day, in the resurrection."

"Martha, I am the resurrection. I am life. Whoever believes in me shall live even though he dies. All who live, all who believe in me and what I am, shall not ever die. Do you believe that?"

"Lord, I believe that you are the Messiah, God's Son who was to come to our age." Then Martha turns and goes to the house to address her sister. "Mary, Mary! The teacher is here. He wants to see you."

When Mary appears we see a sensitive woman whose eyes are hollowed by grief. "Lord, if you had been here our brother would not have died."

Why do we cling to hope when hope is vain? It was too late to say that. Lazarus had died. The "if" is of no use. Yet what else could be said? It was love of life and of Lazarus living that demanded those words. Beyond that vain wish she could only sob and say nothing. Mary and the great rabbi sorrow together for a time before he says quite simply, "Where have you laid him?"

The women of the family respond, for death, like birth, is a matter of which women know most. "Rabbi, come and see," they say and they lead him to the tomb where we await with the dead.

At the entrance to the tomb Jesus stands for a moment. Then, of a sudden, his grief emerges as a sharp and painful cry. Jesus was as vulnerable as they. Overcome by the reality of his friend's death, he grieves with the rest. He weeps. Those around exchange their remarks. "See how much he loved him." "It is hard." "He should have been here sooner. He opened the eyes of the blind. Could he not have kept his friend from dying?" "Do not talk so at a time like this."

Then Jesus steps forward and utters an unthinkable command. "Remove the stone from the tomb!"

Martha cries out in protest. "Oh no, no Lord! He has been dead four days! He will stink!"

"Did I not tell you that if you believed you would see the glory of God?" He spreads his hands skyward in the ancient Jewish gesture of prayer and looks up. "Father, I thank you that you have listened to me all this time. Listen to me now, I pray. This one was mine. These are all mine. You gave them to me and I have taught them as you taught me. Holy Father, keep them and guard them and make them one as we are one."

Now he steps toward the tomb. Sealed for a time, it is now open. He looks into where we, the dead, abide and shouts his command. "Lazarus! Lazarus! Lazarus, come forth!"

What happened in response to this bold command was, of course, the impossible. Lazarus came forth. And at that we find our own reactions radically split. Something in us recoils while another part is inspired. That which recoils says, "No, it should not be. The dead who have died should be left as they are. What has come to rest should be left at rest. Let the dead be honored but, out of honor and respect, let them be dead." The other part cries out, "Let it be so! Let Lazarus live and let all that is dead arise. Let death be no more. Let life be all."

So we love the miracle while we despise it. But our double feelings are the confession that we are the ones—we more than Lazarus—who have been moved. Lazarus simply responds. He walks forth. The truly dead have no recourse but to obey. It is we, the half-dead, who are bothered. We heard the shout that commanded the dead to arise but only half of our existence wanted to obey it or even believe it. The more decent and rational part of us recoiled and said no. Decency demands that what has been buried should be left in its state. So while we want to believe that Lazarus truly arose, truly walked out of the tomb—surely he did, did he not?—the part that recoils refuses to walk forth with him. Yet it is in that dilemma of wanting and not wanting that the sign holds its meaning. It is there that it grips us and demands our response. It is there, in the ambiguity of our present existence, that we can know what it means.

One is tempted to sermonize about it. One is tempted to say that there are unseen shrouds as real as the bands that were wrapped about the body of Lazarus—bands of fear, of selfish blindness, of narrow-mindedness—that there are shrouds of conventionality and respectability that bind us almost as tightly as death and are, therefore, a kind of premature death that defies truly and fully living. One is tempted to speak of those forces that forbid us to live through loving, that forbid us to dare in the face of our doubts. One is tempted to speak of prisons of the soul from which we need to be called forth and to sermonize until we feel shamed for our double nature and particularly ashamed of the rational nature which wants to say an emphatic no to the miracle.

If the tomb in which we dwell is something we have chosen, then we might well feel ashamed. Why, after all, should one choose to die when life is such a wonder and a gift? If all that binds us is our desire to be bound, then we should most cheerfully respond with Lazarus by coming forth. But what if we did not choose? What if the normal circumstances of life simply put us there? Would our ambivalent feelings then be not more than a revelation of the state in which we live—halfway into death at all times and only half alive?

Either way, whether our plight be self-chosen or a fate we could hardly escape, Jesus still beckons in the same manner. The fact is that we do live in semi-darkness if not darkness itself and that death weighs upon us enough to darken our joy. Jesus was that one who sought to live fully in the light and to call us to living there also. He lived and stood for life itself. He challenged all that seeks to overpower that. He struggled, he fought with all that was in him in order that all whom he knew might have life.

The struggle was his own, of course, and not merely a struggle on behalf of others. He too was threatened by death. And in order to finish his course and realize his destiny he had to face death in its fullness. The death of Lazarus, his dear friend, was the ultimate confrontation. If he could not cope with the death of his friend he would not be able to cope with his own. The seventh sign was the last sign needed. It completed the course of his life and readied him for his own personal passion.

Eight

The Passion

Holy Week, we call it. Holy Week, because the things that were done by Jesus during that final week of his terrestrial journey make it holy. This was the week in which he walked steadfastly into the fate he had decided for himself. Or was it the fate decided for him? Both sides of that paradox seem to have been true. He had to decide to do what was decided for him—or so the story is presented in the Gospel according to John. He saw it as something that had to be done, as a script written in advance, as a role that awaited its player. Yet without his decision it could not be.

We have been following Jesus' prophetic career by dramatizing seven episodes of his life. The most dramatic part remains. The events of Holy Week are a drama unto themselves. Leading to the imperial execution on the fateful Friday now called either Good or Black, the drama has the features of a classic Greek tragedy. Just as the *tragos,* an unfortunate goat, was sacrificed in early Greek drama, so would this person die as a sacrifice for his nation.

And then the resurrection turns it all around, turns tragedy to triumph. That, too, is an act unto itself and we shall present it in that manner. To fit the twofold mood of the solemn days of Holy Week we shall try to experience the story as two dramatic episodes to follow the seven we have already been through. The first of these represents the journey that now reaches its destination. The second will be the outcome beyond that destination. But for a certain effect that is hard to capture in the midst of many words, your forbearance is asked to experience this as though you are viewing most of it in silence. Ideally this should be presented as a mimed set of scenes in which we watch familiar material in quietness that demands new thought about the subject. Trying to imagine that, let us read for the sake of silent scenes that mostly speak for themselves. At certain points there is speech to allow Jesus or other characters to say what they must say. It is important that those speeches be heard against the vivid backdrop of the scenery, the pose or the action.

We are at the threshold of the Passover feast. All about the city of Jerusalem and in the villages around, people are making preparations—cleansing their homes, seeing to the purchase of a proper lamb, arranging for family gatherings, bustling about. We are six days before the event, to begin with. We are just outside Jerusalem in the little village of Bethany where Jesus called Lazarus forth from the tomb but a few days ago. The sisters of Lazarus, Martha and Mary, have invited Jesus to a dinner at which he and Lazarus are honored guests. The hostess is Martha. Mary is absent at first. Then she appears to perform a peculiar act of adoration.

She enters with dignity, dressed as for an important occasion. But as she approaches Jesus she loses her composure and begins to weep profusely. She seems to be grieving for the dead as she pours the contents of an expensive bottle of perfume on his feet and then, in a frantic gesture that becomes controlled while she proceeds, dries his feet with her long and glorious hair. She seems to understand something that is puzzling the rest of the company. The act is a lingering ritual of devotion. Surely she senses that he must soon die. Is he going to give his life in exchange for the brother she has just received back from the grave? Or is there another reason?

Her strange deed is interrupted by the man named Judas whom we know as Iscariot—"man of Kerioth." He does not like what she is doing. He is irritated. "This should have been sold for three hundred denarii and the money given to the poor," says he. He tries to stop the woman in this mad devotion, but Jesus restrains him. Jesus is willing to accept what Mary is doing. He who usually showed first concern for the poor is willing to accept an enormously expensive wastage.

We leave this scene behind us as Passover week proceeds. The bustle of activity increases throughout the city of Jerusalem and the countryside. Pilgrims are gathering. The city is fairly swollen with people. But hark! Added to the normal sounds of the occasion we hear cries of *hosanna* and other sounds of what appears to be a political parade! In mimed procession we see Jesus on the back of a donkey, coming into Jerusalem with crowds of people about him, and the people are shouting, shouting, with branches of palms raised on high. "Long live" is the message of the branches. The words they cry are "Save us! Blessings on the King of Israel who comes in the name of the Lord!" (Were we in modern times the branches would be placards with slogans and the slogans would read JESUS FOR KING or JESUS FOR PRESIDENT or OUR NEXT PRESIDENT or even THE MAN WHO WILL SAVE US.) The temple officials come running to the scene as they hear the sounds of the procession. They are alarmed. They are thinking that such a riot can easily bring out the Roman police from the garrison that stood too conveniently close to the holy courts. "You see," they say to each other, "there is nothing you can do. The whole world is running after him."

Jesus moves on and is soon in the center of the city. There he attracts the attention of many, including a group of visiting Greeks, "God-fearers" who have voluntarily embraced the teachings of the Jewish tradition. They approach Jesus' closest companions to request permission for a meeting and Jesus' companions oblige. With country ostentation they lead the Greeks to their master. They attempt an introduction but Jesus seems to ignore their efforts as he turns and speaks his response to the larger audience gathered around.

"So! The hour has come for the Son of Man to be glorified! I tell you most surely, unless the grain of wheat falls into the earth and dies it remains no more than one grain of wheat. But if it dies, it bears much fruit.

"The man who loves his life allows it to be consumed. If he seems to despise his life, he succeeds in becoming eternal.

"If you would serve me, then follow me—for where I am, my servant shall be. But I am alarmed! And what shall I say? Father, preserve me from this hour? No. This is the hour I came for. This is the hour of God's glory." The sounds of an approaching thunderstorm swell beneath these words. The last line is punctuated by a lightning flash and a distant crash of thunder. "I came as light into the world, that whoever has faith in me should not remain in darkness."

Again, we leave a scene behind. Skipping time, we reach the day prior to the Passover and remind ourselves that this is the great memorial feast of the Jewish people. This is the feast at which they recall the exodus, the time when their ancestors were led out of Egypt by Moses to begin their destiny as a nation. It was a feast in which every true son or daughter of Israel was openly and proudly Israelite to the core. Jesus is joining this feast and anticipating it by one day as he gathers his disciples and prepares to dine with them.

As the disciples gather we envision a tableau that reminds us of the scene for the miraculous feeding of the five thousand that we have already beheld. They gather in expectation. They gather as guests. None has considered the need of service until Jesus enters with a towel and a basin. Embarrassment grows as he moves from one to the other, washing their dusty feet. One of them, Peter, is clearly upset. When Jesus gets to him

The Passion

he protests. He will not let his Lord and Master perform so humble a task as to wash his feet. But Jesus insists. If Peter will not allow this, then he will not be truly a part of what Jesus came to accomplish. Once he understands this, Peter offers his hands and his face.But Jesus washes only his feet. Peter has no need for more than this. Then Jesus explains what he has done.

"Do you understand what I have done for you? You call me Lord and Rabbi. If I, your Lord and Rabbi, have washed your feet, you must do the same. For I have given you an example. No servant is greater than his master. Yet, I assure you, anyone who welcomes one whom I send has welcomed me. And whoever welcomes me has welcomed him who sent me."

Jesus seats himself and the meal proceeds. Suddenly he stands and looks about accusingly. All but one of the disciples puzzles and gestures as if to say, "Who? Me?" In a decided movement, Jesus dips a piece of bread into a dish, handing it to the one who did not thus question, the man named Judas Iscariot. Judas appears transformed into something evil. He has suddenly been handed the role of villain in what will turn out to be a terrible drama. He too has been chosen for a role as much as his Lord whom he no longer understands. The man who came for the poor but allowed costly nard to be lavished on his feet by an overwrought woman is seeking to accomplish something strange. He does not understand but he does know his part. The expression on his face turns to pain. "Go," says Jesus. "Do quickly what you are going to do." Then Judas is gone and the sky becomes dark. Jesus speaks to the rest.

"Now is the Son of Man glorified. And God is glorified in him. My little children, I am with you only a little while longer. You shall look for me but where I go you cannot come. Be kind to one another as I have been kind to you. By this you shall be known as my disciples—by your kindness for each other."

"Where are you going, Lord?" asks Peter.

"Where I now go, you cannot follow. But you will follow me later."

"Why can't I follow you now? I would give my life for you!"

"The cock shall not crow before you deny me three times, Peter." He directs his attention to the rest of the group as he continues. "Don't be alarmed. You believe in God. Believe in me. There are many dwelling places in my Father's household. I go to make room for you, that you may be where I am."

Thomas queries him. "We don't know where you are going. How, then, can we know the way?"

"I am the way. I am the truth. I am life. No one approaches the Father except through me." In saying this, Jesus strikes a simple pose that partly bares his breast as though he were saying that he is all men, the Son of Man who truly represents all. They will meet him, you see, in many disguises of neighbors who come to be served, of brothers and sisters with dirty feet, and in those meetings they will again see the way and the truth and life.

"Show us the Father then," says Philip, "and we shall be satisfied."

"Here I am with you all this time and still you don't know me? Whoever has seen me has seen the Father. The Father is glorified in the Son. Ask what you will in my name and I will do it. You shall perform even greater deeds than the deed I have done.

"If you love me, keep my commandments. At my request the Father will send you another advocate—the very Breath of Truth which the world cannot accept because it neither sees nor recognizes. Whoever keeps my commandments is the one who loves me. I will reveal myself to him."

The other Judas speaks up, the Judas whom Luke called the son of James. "How is it that you can reveal yourself to us and not to the world?" he asks.

"Whoever does not love me does not keep my words—and they are words from the One who sent me. I cannot reveal myself to those who don't love me.

"Shalom is my farewell to you. My shalom is my gift to you. And I do not give it as the world gives. Don't be afraid. You have heard me say that I am going away and that I am coming back to you. If you loved me you would rejoice that I am going to the Father, for the Father is greater than I." He turns as though he has heard a sudden sound. "The prince of the world is coming. I can't say much more—though actually he has no hold on me. The world must recognize that I love the Father and do as the Father commands. Get up! Let us be on our way!"

They move away from the table and out into the street as Jesus continues to speak. "I am the vine," he says. "My Father is the gardener who cuts off the branches that bear no fruit. He trims it clean to increase the yield. I am the vine. You are the branches. You must remain attached to me. Remain part of me and what you desire to do shall be done.

"I have loved you with the kindness my Father showed me. Remain in my love by doing my commandments. I say this that you may know the full measure of my joy. This is my commandment: love one another as I have loved you—and no man can have greater love than this, that he lay down his life for those whom he loves."

They stop. Jesus sits and, one by one, they sit as well. "If the world hates you," he continues, "remember this: it hated me first. This world that men have made for themselves has hated me and it shall hate you because you are not a part of it." He stands but motions for his disciples to remain seated. "If I had done no works among them they would not be guilty of sin. But, as it is, they have seen and hated both me and the Father. When the Advocate comes—the Spirit of Truth who comes from my Father—he will bear witness on my behalf." He studies them for a moment or two, as though looking into their futures. "The hour is coming when the man who puts you to death will think that he is serving God. Remember that I told you this.

"In a little while you shall not be able to see me." He looks around. "But then, in another little while, you shall."

Jesus' companions are now very puzzled. They register this by various comments.

"What does he mean?"

"What does he mean by saying 'In a little while you will not see me and then, in another little while, you shall'?"

"Does he intend to go to the Father?"

"What is this 'little while' he speaks of?"

Jesus responds to their various remarks. "Amen! Amen, I say to you! You shall weep and mourn while the world rejoices. You shall be sad but your sadness will turn to joy." He himself seems relieved at having said this. He motions them to rise and they move on as he speaks in a more cheerful tone. "When a woman is in labor she is sad that her hour is come. But when her baby is born, her joy makes her forget the suffering because a baby has been born into the world.

"I talk in figures of speech. A time shall come when I will speak more plainly. The time is coming for you to be scattered—each on his own, leaving me alone. Yet I am not alone, for the Father is with me. I say this to you so that you may have peace. In the world you shall find suffering. But take courage! I have conquered the world."

They have now come to a full stop at a hillside garden that is called Gethsemane. His companions step back as Jesus gets down on his knees and stretches his hands to the sky. He begins to pray and the words we hear are these.

"Father, the hour has come. Glorify your Son that your Son may glorify you. I have glorified you here by finishing the work you gave me to do. Glorify me now with the glory we had before the world came into being.

"I revealed your name to the men you gave me. They were yours but you gave them to me. They have kept your word and have come to know that from you comes all you have given to me. They have believed that you were the One who sent me.

"It is not alone for these that I pray. I pray also for those who shall believe through their witness—that all may be one just as you, Father, and I are one. May the world believe that you sent me! I have given them glory that they may be one just as we are one."

After a time Jesus rises and beckons his companions to come with him. They walk faster now and as they go we can hear the sounds of approaching footsteps and voices. We station ourselves with his disciples as he moves away and is met by a band of policemen. Among them is Judas Iscariot, who comes into our view for only a moment. We hear a dialogue between Jesus and his captors.

"Whom are you seeking?" asks Jesus.

One of the policemen answers. "Jesus the Nazorean."

"I am he." There is no response. "Well, whom do you seek?"

"Jesus the Nazorean," says another policeman quite dumbly.

"I told you that I am he. If I am the one you want, then let these others go." There is a sudden scuffle as Peter rushes into the group that holds Jesus. We hear violent sounds that are suddenly stopped as Jesus commands, "Peter! Put back your sword! Am I not to drink the cup my Father has given me?" At this, Peter and the other companions flee in various directions. We can imagine ourselves either fleeing with them or standing our ground. Whatever we choose to do, we hear the talk of soldiers who are now binding him to take him away. The scene ends with that. In a moment we find ourselves in the temple courtyard or one of the courts around it. A servant girl is tending a charcoal fire there. Peter sneaks in, obviously still trying to stay loyal to his friend and master. He is determined to be as near as he dares. The servant girl studies him for a while, then addresses him. "Are you one of this man's followers?" she asks in a servant's innocence.

Peter responds as though he has been attacked. "Of course not! No ma'am, not me." But coming in over Peter's remark are the sounds that tell us of Jesus' trial.

"Now I must question you about what you do and about those who follow you." The voice is that of a priest. "Tell me . . ."

"I have spoken openly to all the world. I always taught in a synagogue or in the temple courts where all the Jews gather together. There was nothing secret about what I said. Why do you question me? Question those who heard me. They should know what I said." Suddenly we hear a slap on human flesh. Jesus has been struck by one of the temple guards. "Is that any way to answer the high priest?" the man says gruffly.

"If I have done something wrong, then prove it," Jesus retorts. "But if I was right, why strike me?"

Our attention is again back in the court where others have now gathered around Peter and the servant girl, all warming themselves before the fire. "Are you one of his followers?" asks one of the men of Peter.

"No, I'm not," says Peter with more vehemence than seems really necessary.

"Didn't I see you with him in the garden?" The voice has the ominous tone of suspicion. It is one of the policemen who says it. Peter shouts back in a nervous overreaction. "No, I tell you! I was not with this man! I don't even know him." And immediately following his words we hear the pre-dawn crow of a rooster. Peter suddenly catches himself. He grasps his head in his hands and slumps to the ground with a groan.

Jesus has now been moved to another place. He has been sent to Caiaphas, the high priest for that season. The first man who had questioned Jesus was another priest of high rank, a certain Annas who was also the father-in-law of this Caiaphas. One more bit of information about Caiaphas may be valuable. John tells us that he was the one who suggested from the start that Jesus be taken for the sake of the people. "It is better for one man to die for the people," he had said. Realizing the restlessness of the Jerusalem crowds at Passover and the edginess of the Roman occupation police, he was adding in his mind, "than that the people all die for one man."

But there is no real trial at the chambers of Caiaphas. With remarkable prudence, Caiaphas sends Jesus on to the Roman garrison. There, in the early hours of morning, the military governor himself is awakened. Jesus is presented to Pontius Pilate—a Jew handed over by Jews to the man who represented imperial Rome in that part of the world.

Pilate speaks in a heavily sleepy voice that is filled with impatience. "So—what accusation do you bring against this fellow?"

"If he were not an important criminal we certainly wouldn't be bringing him to you at this early hour."

"Well, then, if he is a criminal to you, take him yourselves and judge him by your own law."

"We are not permitted to give a death sentence."

Pilate is taken aback by this. He is suddenly very awake. "O-oh . . . well . . . bring him in." Jesus is brought under guard of several of the temple guards. Pilate looks at the man who is remarkable for his simple appearance. "Are you," says Pilate, "the one they call king of the Jews?"

"Was it your idea to ask or have others told you about me?"

Pilate fairly snorts his reply. "You don't think that I am a Jew? It is your own nation and your own priests who handed you over to me. What have you done?"

"My kingdom is not of this order. If it were, my subjects would fight to save me from being taken. As it is, my kingdom does not belong here."

"So you *are* a 'king'!"

"You say that I am a king. The reason I was born—the reason I came into this order—was to bear witness to the truth. All who belong to the truth listen to my voice."

"Truth?" Pilate fairly spits as he speaks it. "What is truth?" Then the governor leaves Jesus and goes back to the temple delegation that brought this man to him. "I can't make a case against him," he says. "Let's make a deal. It is Passover and you have a custom that we release a prisoner for you at Passover. A political prisoner is what you want, so what say that I release your 'king of the Jews'?"

The protest is abrupt. "No! No, that will not do!" "There is another we would rather have released. There is Barabbas." "Release Barabbas instead."

Pilate leaves this stubborn cadre and walks over to the soldiers who are ever at his beck and call. "Take this fellow out and have him beaten," he barks. "That should satisfy these fools." Pilate is trying to avoid trouble but also a troublesome report to the authorities above him in the imperial system. The soldiers do his bidding. In a moment we hear the measured sounds of a whip on human flesh. For an agonizing time we helplessly listen to this. Then Pilate reappears with the badly bloodied victim beside him. "Look," says Pilate. "I am

The Passion

bringing him out to you to make you understand that I can make no further case against him. Look at the man!"

We look as they must look. What we see is a pitiful sight. His back has been beaten to bloody lacerations. A crown of sharp thorns encircles his head and blood runs down from that. Yet with all that the man named Jesus stands in silent dignity. There have been many like him through history, men beaten for their convictions, but that is the point of it in part. He stands there to represent all who are persecuted for righteousness' sake. Our feelings must surely be feelings of compassion. But those feelings are suddenly overpowered by a cry that screams mad contradiction. "Crucify him! Crucify him! Execute him!" What madness has taken over? The madness of fear, perhaps, for if this man is not sacrificed the entire city if not all the nation may suffer for what he is accomplishing. They are out to save themselves and their people, these men who cry for his blood.

Pilate shouts back fiercely. "Take him yourselves and crucify him! I can't make a sound case against him."

"But we have our law too and by our law he should die because he pretended to be God's Son—a Messiah!"

Pilate is sobered by that. He knows little enough about the Jews but he has heard that their "Son of God" was a long awaited king. He can't afford to take chances. There may be the seed of an insurrection in this man's following after all. He speaks to Jesus again. "Where do you come from?" There is no response. "You refuse to speak to me now? Don't you know that I can release you—or have you crucified?"

Jesus' answer is simple but strong. "You would have no power over me at all if it were not given to you from above."

The voices of Jesus' accusers rise to overpower this little dialogue. "If you free this fellow you are not a Friend of Caesar," they shout. "Any man who pretends to be king becomes the emperor's rival. Do you like your job enough to keep it?" Laughter of a vicious sort follows this last line.

Pilate once again leads Jesus before them. He is threatened by what they have said. He is angry. He shouts at the top of his voice. "Look! Here is your king!"

"Away with him! Away with him! Execute him your Roman way!"

"Shall *I* execute *your* king?"

"We have no king but Caesar!"

Surely they can't have meant it? But they have said it. And what they have said is too much for further response from Pilate. He is the one who should have spoken their last line. But they have said it and that leaves him no recourse. If he would save his office and the authority of the empire, he must do as they have cried. Jesus is led away to be prepared for execution.

What follows is too familiar to require staging. We know it too well, for we have heard of it often. Or if we should try to stage it we would not be able. Any attempt would fall short of doing justice to what is too sacred for words. There are details to be noted. He was executed on a knoll called the Place of the Skull, he and two others. Placed above him on the cross was the inscription, "Jesus the Nazorean, the King of the Jews." It was written in Hebrew and Latin and Greek. The Jewish chief priests objected to this but Pontius Pilate, realizing what little triumph he could out of the matter, replied, "What I have written, that I have written." His clothing was divided among the soldiers who had stripped him. He died naked. His mother was there and two other women. So also was a certain disciple he loved very much. As he died he turned to that one and to his mother and said, "Woman, look at your son." Then, to that one he said, "Here is your mother." This summarized his teaching in a simple way. He had come to be brother and sister to all that all might be children of God together. Every mother could be every son's mother and every son a son to every woman.

"I am thirsty," Jesus cried at the last. An ironic cry, that cry. He had been water of life to others but now he was in need of it himself. They quenched his thirst with wine soaked into a sponge. He sucked it and then simply said, "It is finished." With that he died.

He was buried in the grave of a wealthy man, a Jew named Joseph of Arimathea. With that man to help in the burial was another Pharisee, a certain Nicodemus who had once come to him by night. They wrapped his body with cloths and mortuary spices and ointment. They too were leaders of the Jerusalem Jews, but of a sort that honored him well and followed his ways.

There are songs to be sung at this solemn moment. There are many that express feelings that need expression. From the many the author suggests one from the American black tradition.

> Oh, they whupped him up the hill,
> up the hill, up the hill.
> Oh, they whupped him up the hill
> and he never said a mumblin' word.
> He just hung down his head and he cried.

> Oh, they tied him to the tree,
> to the tree, to the tree.
> Oh, they tied him to the tree
> and he never said a mumblin' word.
> He just hung down his head and he cried.

Oh, they pierced him in the side,
in the side, in the side.
Oh, they pierced him in the side
and he never said a mumblin' word.
He just hung down his head and he died.

Nine

Resurrection Morn

The four New Testament Gospels have four varying accounts of Jesus' rising. The secretive account of Mark contrasts with the sensational account in Matthew that includes an earthquake. There are disagreements on the number of men or angels at the tomb, with two accounts presenting one and the other giving us two. There is lack of agreement on the number of women who went to the tomb and who they were. Yet in the midst of the variant accounts two items of information are to be found in all four: an empty tomb and the presence of Mary Magdalene.

In John's Gospel these two features are in central focus.

The beginning of the final episode as seen by John has none of the fanfare with which exuberant Christians now greet the Easter dawn. There are no trumpets, there is no rolling of drums. There is only the hush of a grief-ridden night giving way to the pre-dawn light. It was very early and still dark, writes the evangelist, when Mary of Magdala came to the tomb.

What we first see, then, is a very sad woman, a woman whose hope and love have been crushed, walking to the place where Nicodemus and Joseph had laid him whom she had followed. Did she go to pay some last respects or to do something additional for his mortal remains? We do not know.

As we watch her we see her suddenly arrested in her heavy-hearted step. She looks up, sees that the stone no longer stands against the entrance to the tomb, turns and runs away.

Breathlessly she approaches two of the apostles she has learned to trust, Peter and the disciple who is never named but always called the one whom Jesus loved. Breathlessly she cries, "They have taken the Lord out of the tomb!"

Can we sense the alarm that filled the mind of the woman, the fear that caused her to suspect an anonymous "they" who would do such a thing as to take her master's body away? In her devotion she had come to love this man. Now all that was left for her to love was a body recently buried in a tomb. All her feelings were attached to that body and that body was gone. Her cry was the cry of one twice betrayed. Not only had her great friend's life been cut short; "they" had now also taken all that was left to take.

Alarmed by her report the two men hastened to the tomb to see for themselves. The quietness of early dawn has now turned to excitement and concern. The tomb is indeed empty, and to add to the puzzle, the linen wrappings of the corpse are on the ground. Only the cloth that had covered the head is neatly rolled up as though it were quite deliberately and reverently laid there by one who cared.

The men are satisfied that Mary's report is true. The tomb is empty. The body is gone. They must now tell the others and so they depart.

Everything else that happens at the scene happens only to Mary Magdalene. She was alone. She alone saw Jesus and took him to be the gardener. Or did she see a gardener who suddenly became Jesus to her? We must trust Mary's memory, for we have nothing else as testimony for us.

We see her outside the tomb weeping. When her two friends departed she dared to step into the tomb itself and there she sees two messengers clad in white, one sitting at the head of where the body had been, the other at the feet.

"Woman, why are you weeping?" they say. In utter simplicity and with no sign of amazement at the appearance of angels she answers, "They have taken my Lord away and I don't know where they have put him."

Mary is a wounded woman. Nothing but her loss occupies her mind. Confused by all else, she turns around and sees the man whom she takes to be the gardener. "Woman, why are you weeping?" he asks—the very same question as that of the two messengers. "Whom are you looking for?"

"Sir," she says, "if you have taken him away, tell me where you have put him and I will remove him."

She knows that her friend had no pre-cut tomb of his own. Perhaps those Pharisees, Joseph and Nicodemus, had changed their minds about letting him lie there—or somehow had put him into the wrong tomb! Never mind. She could take care of that. Her devotion would give her the strength to move his body to wherever it must be moved. She would take care of that.

But the gardener knows her. He is not one of the "they" who have removed her dear Lord and Friend. "Mary," he says.

At that she sees him to be the very one whose absence she grieves. "Rabbuni!" she cries ("*My* Lord," it means) and throws her arms about him.

In contrast to the raising of Lazarus this is almost anti-climactic. There is no loud command to call forth a corpse from the tomb. There is no earthquake to announce the event as in Matthew. There is only the quietness of the early morn after the sabbath and this personal meeting.

The gentleness and unspectacular character of it recall the simple saying with which Jesus had announced his destiny: unless a grain of wheat falls into the ground and dies it remains only a single grain; but if it dies it yields a rich harvest. The kernel of wheat had fallen. Now it was rising, as strongly but gently as the first green blade after planting. The blade would appear to others—to the gathered disciples, to Thomas, to Simon Peter. But there would be no great triumphal procession, no grand proclamation to the world. All that would come later. Here, at the first, only the eyes of those who had been trained to see were able to see him risen. Essentially it was a quiet mystery, the mystery of an empty tomb and a reunion with a dear friend named Mary. From that gentle beginning all else would derive.

It was the dying that had been difficult and dramatic. The rising came easy. Casting the seed into the ground had been hard. Deciding to let it fall had been the agony. Now that it had fallen, life had taken care of itself. As ever before and as it ever shall be, life had taken over where death left off. Life had swallowed death. Life had overcome.

> Now the green blade rises from the buried grain
> Wheat that in the dark earth many days has lain
> Love lives again that with the dead has been
> Love is come again like wheat arising green.
>
> In the grave they laid him, love by hatred slain
> Thinking that he would never wake again
> Laid in the earth like grain that sleeps unseen
> Love is come again like wheat arising green.
>
> Forth he came at Easter like the risen grain
> He that for three days in the grave had lain
> Raised from the dead my living Lord is seen
> Love is come again like wheat arising green.
>
> When our hearts are wintry, grieving as in pain
> Your touch can call us back to life again
> Fields of our hearts that dead and bare have been
> Love is come again like wheat arising green.
> *An Old French Carol*

Supplement

Directions for Staging as Chancel Drama

When the author first set out to write this work he had in mind an actual play that could be produced on stage or as a series of chancel dramas. The first draft of the book became, in fact, just that. But there were problems with it. In order to carry that off successfully the author and others felt that it needed to depart more than it did from the text of John's Gospel. For various reasons that seemed undesirable.

To retain the possibility of still doing it as chancel drama but to write a book primarily for readers and for a certain season, the present format was chosen. For those who wish to try chancel drama based on this text, this supplement is added. The directions presented here are far from prescriptive. They are, rather, quite open and not much more than suggestive. Because sanctuaries and chancels vary much in design it was considered best to keep it that way. This means that anyone who tries to produce the material will have to be creative in a number of ways.

The dialogue for the dramas is worked into the text as transparently as possible. At certain points a narrator is needed. At other points the staging and acting can take care of what is narrated in the text. Pencilling through a copy of the book will be the beginning of the process.

Two major points of direction are of utmost importance. One is that the person of Jesus must be a trained actor who has the strength and appearance needed for such a demanding role. He should be about thirty. He should be lean but of any height. If possible, a man of dark coloring and imaginably Jewish appearance should be chosen. His quality of strength must come from within. It must be the strength of silence that becomes all the stronger when he breaks out of that silence into speech.

The second most important point of direction is to realize the importance of staging and setting. Properties and scenery must be minimal but they must also be artistically conceived and designed. Costuming is a matter of considerable option. One could strive for a first-century look with flowing skirts and robes over brief, kilt-like undergarments. Preferable, perhaps, is totally contemporary dress. Choosing modern costumes to fit each character could be quite a lot of fun. Jesus would, of course, have to be quite country in appearance.

A good narrator will be essential. To lend continuity to the series we suggest that the narrator read the prologue material ("The Prelude to the Signs") as an introduction to each presentation.

For further suggestions we proceed scene by scene.

One: The Sign of the Wine

There is no way to do this scene without a large group of people. All the extras available can be placed in all available space. Only Jesus, Mary, the bride and groom with parents, the steward of the feast, the household servants and a few of Jesus' companions need to be identifiable.

Most crucial to the set are the six large water jars. They can be made of lightweight material but should represent a capacity of thirty gallons each. The shape should be simple: fairly tall, somewhat bulbous cylinders. Vessels for filling and for the serving of water become wine can be some shape of pitchers—pottery of course.

All the action and whatever music might be chosen to enhance it must suggest not only a wedding but a wedding that is boisterously joyful when it is in full swing. The point of the drama is the near loss and then the recovery of the joy. Dance will be a most fitting culmination of the scene.

Two: The Sign of the Temple

Recreating some kind of replica of the Jerusalem temple is out of the question. But what better suggestion could we have than whatever church chancel is available? All that we need to do to communicate the incongruity of matters is to introduce merchants and moneychangers into the chancel. Crates of live chickens and pigeons would be marvelously effective. Larger animals might present difficulties, though a few lambs in a floored pen are possible.

Noisiness is essential. A cacophony of merchants' cries against a background of sacred chants will be most effective.

For the scene with Nicodemus all that will have to recede. Soft light surrounding the two characters in clear, simple focus will be ideal. The privacy of the conversation and the importance of every line of speech are primary elements of this second scene. Only a sense for that will give this scene the strength that it needs to supersede the boisterous scene with which the episode begins.

A soft rendition of such a simple melody as the Church's ancient "Of the Father's Love Begotten" would be a suitable musical addition.

In the first episode Jesus was persuaded by his mother to try his God-given powers. In this scene he discovers them for himself. It must have been a heady and frightening experience. Exhilaration and anger can show together in the temple scene. Some of that should remain in his eyes as he shares some of the secrets of his power with the open-minded Nicodemus.

Three: The Sign of the Well

It is important that an outdoor effect be created for the staging of this episode. This can be accomplished in various ways. A scene of the Samaritan hills could be projected on whatever flat surfaces are available, even if the projection spills from one surface to another. In addition to that or without it, greenery and small trees can be placed about a replica of a stone well that is the one essential set piece for the encounter and dialogue between Jesus and the Samaritan woman.

Whoever is chosen to play the woman should be a strong character. She must begin the dialogue as his apparent equal in strength of personality.

One might think it difficult to perform this without the use of first century garb because of the fact that a woman fetching water at a well is clearly an ancient scene. Yet a woman in simple country dress of our time might be effective in a certain way that is both delightful and significant. In similar country dress the two lead characters can be a convincing pair.

A somewhat altered version of an old folk hymn might serve as helpful musical accompaniment for this scene. A choir or soloist could sing the following text at the conclusion or at the beginning of the scene as well.

Jerusalem, my happy home,
when shall I come to thee?

When shall my sorrows have an end,
Thy joys when shall I see?

Jerusalem, my happy home,
would God I were in thee!
Would God my woes were at an end,
thy joys that I might see!

Jerusalem, what came of thee?
Thy walls no longer stand.
While thy stones crumble into the dust
I wander through the land.

Jerusalem, I leave thee lie
upon thy bed of stone
While I, the wanderer, seek my God
where all the world is home.

(The copyright for the familiar folk tune is owned by J. Fisher and Brothers.)

Four: The Sign of the Healer

As in the second episode, we here must cope with the need for two scenes. A few people and some greenery around Jesus, all placed off to one side of the main playing area is all that is needed for the first scene, which is brief. In some sanctuaries a balcony or choir loft or some similar architectural feature can serve well. From this area Jesus and his followers can then move to the main stage which must represent a pool in Jerusalem. Some semblance of stone walls could help to effect this scene, or an actual scene of the present Old City of Jerusalem projected on wall space. In some way a pool with a stone pavement around must be constructed. Building a platform around a lower area such as the front of the nave is a ready possibility. (In a Baptist edifice, the baptismal pool could be ideal.)

Because the theme is man's conduct on the sabbath, traditional sabbath music could provide effective accompaniment, or whatever music suggests the Lord's Day to a given audience.

By this time Jesus seems quite assured of his power. The first healing is one of many. Against that background Jesus was able to merely tell the man by the pool to get up and walk if he is willing. The full power of his presence is in the brief command. That same sense of assured power must emerge in his verbal contest with the guardians of the sabbath.

Five: The Sign of Bread

Because this episode is about the Eucharist it will be important to set the stage so as to suggest that. The people who represent the five thousand could be crowded around the Communion rail or gathered where the congregation normally gathers for the Lord's Supper. Yet because the original scene was in the open country, some representation of that is also in order. As suggested previously, a scene of a hillside—even a Palestinian hillside—can be projected on wall space.

A strong musical suggestion of place can be given by the use of such a pair of familiar hymns as "I Walked Today Where Jesus Walked" and "O Bread of Life from Heaven."

The illusion of multiplying loaves and fish can be accomplished in more than one way. The people can merely mime the eating and their satisfaction. If the backs of the group are to the audience as when they are gathered at the Communion kneeler, there is no problem at all.

To accomplish the second scene, Jesus and his companions only have to move out of the center of the chancel to another stage. Disappearing out of two separate doors to fit what is suggested by the script is simple. The crowd can follow in part alone and appear shortly after.

The character playing Jesus is now playing a man whose power seems to have gotten out of hand. It is causing problems. People want what he has to give for the wrong reasons, or want something other than what he wants to give. This should cause him to project a sense of concern that borders on worry. He is struggling to communicate hard lessons to an audience that cannot or will not fully understand him. Note that some of his followers decide to leave him at the end of this episode. This must appear to be a logical or sensible thing to do.

Six: The Sign of Sight

Whatever was used to represent Jerusalem in the third episode can be used here again. This is the second of three times that Jesus confronts the population of that city. With each meeting that city's leaders become more determined to get rid of him. This scene represents the midpoint of the tension that forms in that particular conflict.

What is unique about this scene is that for much of it the attention is not directly on Jesus. Rather, it is on a dialogue between the man born blind and Jesus' opponents. If it is done well, that dialogue should be humorous. At the beginning the man born blind is at the bottom. He is a lowly, sinful (his blindness proves it) beggar. At the end he has been exalted as the one who truly sees while his critics are accused of being blind. That victory should bring sincere delight to the audience. A fairly harsh, judgmental Jesus makes that pronouncement. The tension in the conflict becomes quite alarming at this turn. Jesus' exit should be a true escape for his life. Music chosen for the scene should heighten this growing tension and sharp departure.

Seven: The Sign of the Tomb

This is the most challenging episode of them all. For the most effective results the staging should be so managed that the audience is given the sense of being in the tomb where Lazarus will be deposited. Visually, such an illusion could be created by constructing a replica of a stone opening to be set up in center stage, front. Though a bit costly, a weblike construction of black netting could be made to emanate from that arched opening to separate the audience from the actors. At the point where Lazarus is buried a shrouded body—or a casket if one wants a modern touch—should be carried through the opening and laid in the area where the audience is seated. Much can be done with lighting. An appropriate mood in sound can be set with portions of J. S. Bach's "Christ Lag in Todesbunden."

As with other episodes, more than one scene is called for. If possible, perform with sound only in the action that takes place away from the tomb. The sounds of the speech of Jesus and his companions can come from various unseen locations to give the sense of distance.

For Jesus' own career, this scene is climactic. Everything important hinges on it. If he cannot cope with the death of his friend Lazarus, then the journey cannot continue. This is the ultimate test of his power. He must be able to call Lazarus from the tomb or he will not be able to go to his own death with the hope that he needs. The actor who plays Jesus' part must lay it all on the line in this scene. And what happens for him must happen for the audience. We need to be profoundly moved by this last "sign." In the original drama script that was written, the following directions were given. They assume a fairly elaborate set but may communicate what is needed if that can be overlooked.

The lights go down to darkness and the words of Jesus echo as though through the chambers of a catacomb as Jesus calls out, "Lazarus! Lazarus! Lazarus, come forth!" When the echo of the sounds have died away we hear the sound of falling chains followed by measured footsteps. Suddenly there is a crash of light and sound. The net is gone and the stage is filled with people who are dancing and singing. In the midst of the merriment and the movement we see a few washing the feet of their neighbors.

In a chancel setting the joy might have to be more sedate than this. Joyful music on a pipe organ would be appropriate, especially if the theme is recognizably Easter. Dance that echoes the dance of the wedding feast would have a powerful effect.

Eight: The Passion

This is the lengthiest of the episodes and the most complex to be staged. At the beginning, where much must be mimed, a series of vignettes might be easiest and also most effective. With little or no stage set we can successively behold the scenes of Mary washing the feet of Jesus with her tears, the parade with the palm branches, the gathering for the Supper and the washing of feet, and the move to the garden where he is betrayed. Perhaps the garden can be made as a special set. It can be very effective if it echoes the scene of Jesus' dialogue with Nicodemus from the second episode. The courtyard, where Peter warms his hands by the fire and betrays his

Lord, is a second set that is needed. It can be as simple as a glowing fire of coals and some stones to represent the inner corner of a wall. Much of the "action" must be done with sound only from offstage while this scene is in focus. After the beating at the hands of the soldiers Jesus should appear. This need not be a bold appearance. Visionlike, in subdued light, it might be more effective than under a harsh spotlight. A subdued effect is preferable to something too melodramatic. Note that the narration pictures him as standing in silent dignity. The cries to crucify him might be all the more effective if they come from behind the audience or even from where the audience is seated. As Jesus is led away he need only disappear in a fading of light. At that point all might be best communicated with simple symbolism. Because a cross is a very powerful sign in and of itself, a lightweight cross of large proportion might be raised slowly within sight of the audience. I would recommend no effort to depict the body hanging on it but simply JESUS THE NAZOREAN, THE KING OF THE JEWS inscribed upon it. Good Friday music done by choir or organ can handle the rest but let it be subdued. A particular folk hymn is suggested in the script.

Nine: Resurrection Morn

Since this would be done on Easter morning itself there could be no better setting than the traditional bank of lilies. A replica of the opening to the tomb would be in order. The flowers could be placed to lend focus to that. Simplicity and quietness are important. The struggle is over. The miracle took place in our absence and without our noticing. The true surprise of it all is the ease with which life triumphed. The person who plays Mary Magdalene must be a strong and powerfully sensitive character. We must be given the feeling that she is stronger than she feels herself to be. Jesus will, after all, disappear and she will be on her own. We must know that she can make it from there on with strength. The dialogue between her and her Master should be strong in its simplicity, its sincerity and its warmth. If done well it should be an immensely comforting scene.

We strongly recommend the use of the hymn text written in the script. A choir or soloist could sing it or part of it first. It would be very good if the audience could join the action by singing it at least in part.